Understand Networking

-: Authors :-

Ms. Miral Kothari

Ms. Ripal Ranpara   Ms. Nehal Dave

ISBN-13: 978-1722683573

Title ID: 8767710

Table of Contents

Acknowledgement

We would like to express our gratitude to the many people who saw us through this book; to all those who provided support and offered comments.

We would like to give special thanks to the Honourable Secretary P.P. Sadhu Tyagvallabhdas of Yogidham Gurukul for his continuous shower of blessings.

We also take this opportunity to thank the Principal Shree M. & N. Virani Science College Dr. K. D. Ladva for their guidance and support.

We also thank to Head of computer science department Dr. Stavan Patel and Dr. Hitendra Donga for their motivational support.

We would like to thank our family members who supported and encouraged us all the time.

Last but not the least: We beg forgiveness of all those who have been with us over the journey and whose names we have failed to mentio

What is communication?

- o Communication is a process which is used by any entity to express its thoughts or feelings.
- o Communication can be done between minimum two entities.

So, to communicate we need:

- o Two or more than two parties
- o Transmitter
- o Media
- o Receiver

Communication Model

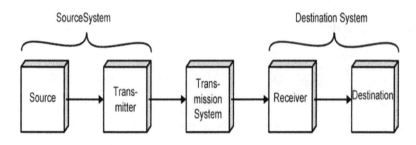

(a) General block diagram

- o Source
  - o It is a place where the data to be transferred is obtained from user
- o Transmitter
  - o It transmits data to the receiver
- o Transmission medium
  - o It is used for transmission of data on defined path of network
- o Receiver
  - o It will obtain the data from transmission medium
- o Destination
  - o It will receive the data and will generate or show the output

What is network?

- o In simple words, a network consists of two or more computers that are linked with each other.
- o It is the practice of linking two or more computing devices together for the purpose of sharing data.
- o Networks are built with a mix of computer hardware and computer software.

Why to establish a network?
- o Communication
- o Sharing resources
- o Exchange information

- In information technology, a network is a series of points or **nodes interconnected** by communication paths.
- To enable the communication, the computers on a network **need a medium.**
- So, they may be linked through *cables, telephone lines, radio waves, satellites, or infrared light beams.*
- So, the ultimate purpose of a network is to enable the sharing of files and information between multiple systems.

Information or data can be shared in two ways:
- Local sharing
- Remote sharing

Effectiveness of data communication depends on:
1. Delivery – Data should be delivered at correct destination.
2. Accuracy – Only demanded data should be delivered.
3. Timeliness– Data should be delivered within reasonable time limit.

Dataflow:
> The manner in which data transmission is done
- **Simplex**

- o Simplex data flow is unidirectional transmission.
- o It can use entire capacity of the channel
- o **Half duplex**
  - o In this, both the sender and the receiver can transmit but not at the same time.
  - o The entire capacity of the channel can be used by transmitter (sending the message).
- o **Full duplex**
  - o In this, both the transmitter can transmit and receive at the same time.
  - o Here, the signals share the capacity of the channel
- o **Factors affecting data flow**
  - o Cost
    - More complex technologies are more expensive
  - o Size of bandwidth
    - Full duplex communication requires greater bandwidth
  - o Use of bandwidth
    - In half duplex communication, bandwidth may be wasted during intervals.

Network Services
- o In computer networking, a **network service** is a

- o data storage,
- o manipulation,
- o presentation,
- o communication or
- o other capability

Which is often implemented based on network protocols running at the application layer of a network.

1. File Service

- o On network it is possible to share files and directories over the network using the Network File System (NFS).
- o It allows a user on a client computer to access files over a network in a manner similar to how local storage is accessed.
- o From the point of view of file sharing, the computer which gives access to its files and directories is called the *server*, and the computer using these files and directories is the *client*.
- o It includes all the network functions dealing with the storage, retrieval or movements of data files.

2. Print Service

- o This service allows you to print a job DIRECTLY to a network printer from your network connected PC.

- A job of any size can be sent from ANY application resident on your PC.
- As an administrator of network, you need to do two main things so users throughout a network can access print devices connected to workstation or server:
    - you need to set up a workstation or server as a print server
    - you need to use the print server to share print devices on the network.
- Many users can share the same printer which is an expensive device.
- Printers can be located anywhere in the network.

3. Communication Service
- Communication service allows members of the network to communicate with each other.
- As communication is one of the main purposes of the network, every member of the network must be able to communicate with remaining member of the network.
- Areas:
    - Voice mail, Fax service, E-mail

4. Database Service
- A database service can serve highly-available data to a database application.

o The application can then provide network access to database client systems.

o A database service on network allows the members of the network to access the same data at multiple ends and to modify or delete the data from database if authenticated.

5. Security Service

o One of the important services is security service on network.

o Network provides security options at different levels

o The purpose of network is to make the resources easily accessible.

o But administrators always have to worry about unauthorized access.

  o Elements of network security
    o Authentication
    o Access permissions
    o Password protected sharing

6. Application service

o Application Network Services adds intelligence to your *network* to recognize, route, or transform application messages, all with trusted security.

o Application service on network offers application to be accessed from various point of network.

Network / Channel Access Methods
- o Rules for access, transmit and release the channel
- o Sharing rules:
    - o First come, first serve
    - o Take turns

3 basic channel access methods:
- o Contention
- o Polling
- o Token passing

Contention Based Access Methods
- o First come first serve
- o Equal access rights to all stations
- o Transmitting station is non-concern with other stations
    - o So, more than one station transmit at the same time and result into collision
- o Solutions to reduce collision are:
    - o Carrier sensing (listen before talking)
    - o Carrier detection (listen also while talking)
- o Specifications to avoid collision will introduce:
    - o **CSMA/CD** and **CSMA/CA**

- o **CSMA/CD**
    - o Carrier Sense Multiple Access with Collision Detection

- o Carrier sensing and detection together form a protocol
- o Limits of network to 2500 meters
- o Longer distance – no sensing of two ends
- o **CSMA/CA**
  - o Carrier Sense Multiple Access with Collision Avoidance
  - o Additional technique to reduce collision
  - o System signals a warning – others will wait
    - Increases traffic
    - Listening to warnings increases system load
- o **Polling Access Method**
  - o Designates one device as a channel access administrator
  - o The administrator addresses a request to the secondary system for data and then receives the data.
  - o The administrator then polls another secondary.
- o **Token Passing System**
  - o A small frame is passed in an orderly fashion from one device to another.
  - o Each device knows from which device it receives the token and to which device it passes the token.

o Each system retransmits the token for the next device.

Network Models:

1. Client – Server :

o The **client–server model** is a distributed application structure that partitions tasks or workloads between the providers of a resource or service, called servers, and service requesters, called clients.

o A server is a host that is running one or more server programs which share their resources with clients.

o A client does not share any of its resources, but requests a server's content or service function.

o Clients therefore initiate communication sessions with servers which await incoming requests.

o The client–server model was developed at Xerox PARC during the 1970s.

Advantages:

o Single point of storage
o Centralized administration
o Easy to manage and maintain the resources
o Easy up-gradation and installation
o Security can be maintained easily.

2. Peer – to – peer network :

o In its simplest form, a peer-to-peer (P2P) network is created when two or more PCs are connected and share resources without going through a separate server computer.

o A P2P network can be an ad hoc connection—a couple of computers connected via a Universal Serial Bus to transfer files.

o In effect, every connected PC is at once a server and a client.

o There's no special network operating system residing on a robust machine that supports special server-side applications like directory services (specialized databases that control who has access to what).

o In a P2P environment, access rights are governed by setting sharing permissions on individual machines.

Topology

Bus Topology:
   o The bus topology consists of computers connected by a single cable called a backbone.
   o In a bus environment, 10Base2 or 10Base5 cable is used.
      o As all devices share the same bandwidth, the more devices the slower the network.
   o It is not feasible for more than 10 workstations.
   o In a bus topology, computers only listen for data being sent to them... they do not forward data.
      o This is called Passive topology.

- A general signal moves from one end of the bus to the other end.
- If it is not stopped, it will continue bouncing back and forth.
- To prevent this, a terminator is located at each end of the cable.

Ring Topology:
- In a ring topology, each computer connects directly to the next one in line, forming a circle.
- Data travels in a clockwise direction, and each computer accepts the information intended for it and passes on the information for other computers.
- It uses a token, which is actually a small packet, to send information.

Star Topology:
- In a star topology, the computers are connected to a centralized hub by a cable segment.
- They require more cabling than ring or bus topologies.
- In this topology each computer is connected to the hub by its own cable.
  - Therefore, if connection of one computer goes down then it does not affect the rest of the network.

o Because each workstation has its own connection.

Mesh Topology
o In mesh topology, all devices are connected to each other more than once to create fault tolerance.
o A single device or cable failure will not affect the performance because the devices are connected by more than one means.
o More expensive

Ethernet
o It is a system for connecting a number of computer systems to form a local area network, with protocols to control the passing of information and to avoid simultaneous transmission by two or more systems.

CDDI
o Copper Distributed Data Interface
o It is a standard for data transmission that uses shielded twisted-pair (STP) or unshielded twisted pair (UTP) copper wire.

FDDI
o FDDI (Fiber Distributed Data Interface) is a standard for data transmission on fiber optic lines in a local area network (LAN).

- It can extend in range up to 200 km (124 miles).
- The FDDI protocol is based on the token ring.
- FDDI local area network can support thousands of users.

Communication methods
- Unicasting : One to one
- Multicasting : One to many
- Broadcasting : One to all

Network models and LAN sharing

OSI reference model

- o Open System Interconnection
- o It was first released in 1984 by ISO (International Standards Organization)
- o It provides a useful structure for defining and describing the various processes.
- o It organizes communication protocols into seven layers.

THE 7 LAYERS OF OSI

TRANSMIT   RECEIVE

DATA   USER   DATA

Application layer

Presentation layer

Session layer

Transport layer

Network layer

Data link layer

Physical layer

PHYSICAL LINK

Seven layers of OSI model

- Application layer
- Presentation layer
- Session layer
- Transport layer
- Network layer
- Data link layer
- Physical layer

- Away
- Pizza
- Stale
- Throw
- Not
- Do
- Please

- **Physical layer**
  - It transmits bits over the network media.
  - It provides physical connection among the network devices.
  - It transmits 1's and 0's only
  - It establishes and maintains physical connection.
- **Data link layer**
  - It is responsible for
    - error notification,
    - ordered delivery of frames and
    - flow control
  - At the sending end, it handles conversion of data into raw formats that can be handled by the physical layer.

- o It is divided into 2 sub layers:
    - o MAC (Media Access Control) (for physical addressing)
    - o LLC (Logical Link Control) (data link connection between network devices)
- **Network layer**
  - o It is responsible for routing.
  - o It accepts messages from source and converts them to packets.
  - o It is responsible for best route.
  - o If many packets are in the network at the same time, it is controlled by the network layer.
- **Transport layer**
  - o It provides transport service between Session layer & Network layer.
  - o It takes information from Session layer, splits up and send it to network layer.
  - o It checks information arrived successfully on the destination.
  - o It requests for retransmission of data if not received.
  - o It keeps track of packet sequence numbers.
- **Session layer**
  - o It manages dialogues.
  - o It establishes connection, maintains connection and terminates connection that

means it allows users to establish connections between devices.

o Once connection is established, both parties are enabled to communicate.

o Applications on either ends of the session are able to exchange data for the duration of session.

- **Presentation layer**
  o It manages data structures and conversion.
  o It converts the data from the representation used inside the computer to the network standard representation.
  o If any packets is lost during the travelling, then it will send a sign to the sender that it requires the specific packet.
  o It is responsible for encryption, decryption, compression, decompression etc.

- **Application layer**
  o This layer is interface between the user's application and the network.
  o It helps transferring a file between two different systems that require handling and other incompatibilities.

Transmission Media

Transmission medium

o It is the physical path between transmitter and receiver in a data transmission system.

There are two types of transmission medium

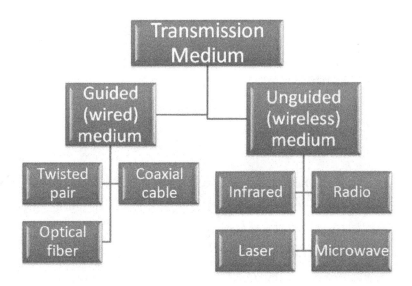

Transmission frequencies

o The transmission of data is possible only because of transmission media.

o Transmission is being done by electronic signals in the form of binary impulses.

o Computers always transmit signals in form of electromagnetic (EM) wave form.

o Depending on the frequency of EM waves, different media are used.

Frequency:
o When electrons move, they create electromagnetic waves that can propagate through free space.
o The number of oscillation (swinging) of an electromagnetic wave is called its frequency.

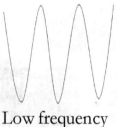 

Low frequency   High frequency

o Radio frequency waves often are used for LAN signaling. They can be transmitted using coaxial or twisted pair cable.
o Microwave transmissions can be used to communicate between earth stations and satellites. Cellular phone networks are examples of systems that use low-power microwave signals.

Attenuation:
- o It is a measure of how much a signal weakens as it travels through a medium.
- o Difficult to isolate original signal
  - o E.g. Radio

Immunity from EMI:
- o Electromagnetic Interference (EMI) consists of outside electromagnetic noise that distorts the signal in a medium.
  - o E.g. Crosstalk

Coaxial cable
- o Coaxial cable gets its name – two conductors that are parallel to each other, or on the same axis.
- o Support 10 to 100 mbps of bandwidth.

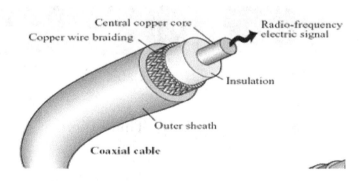

Central copper core
Copper wire braiding
Radio-frequency electric signal
Insulation
Outer sheath
Coaxial cable

Components of coaxial cable
- o Central conductor: usually solid copper wire, made up of stranded wire.
- o Outer conductor: consists of braided wires, metallic foil or both – shield – serves as ground – protects the inner conductor from EMI
- o Insulation layer: keeps the outer conductor spaced from inner conductor. (non conductive material)
- o Plastic encasement (jacket): protects the cable from damage.
- o Single cable failure take down an entire network down. One piece of cable is broken; the entire segment will stop working.

Categories of coaxial cable

Category	Use
RG – 59	Cable TV
RG – 58	Thin Ethernet
RG - 11	Thick Ethernet

- o Thinnet:
    - o 0.25 inches (6 mm) thickness
    - o Transmit a signal for 185 meters (610 feet)
- o Thicknet:
    - o 0.5 inches (13 mm) thickness
    - o Transmit a signal for 500 meters (1650 feet)
    - o It is sometimes called standard Ethernet.

Twisted pair cable
- o Most popular type, light weight, easy to install, inexpensive
- o Made up of solid copper twisted around each others.
- o Can be used for analog/digital transmission
- o Two varieties of twisted pair cable:
    - o Unshielded twisted pair
    - o Shielded twisted pair

1. Unshielded Pair Cable (UTP)
- o It does not incorporate a braided shield
- o Several twisted pairs bundled together in a single cable
- o Used for voice or data applications.
- o UTP consists of 2 or 4 pairs of twisted pair cables:
    - o 2 pairs use RJ - 11
    - o 4 pairs use RJ – 45

- Easy to install
- Comes in 5 categories

2. Shielded Twisted Pair

- STP consists more twisted pair – enclosed in a foil wrap copper shielding.
- The extra shield protects from EMI
- Comes in 5 types for different purposes.

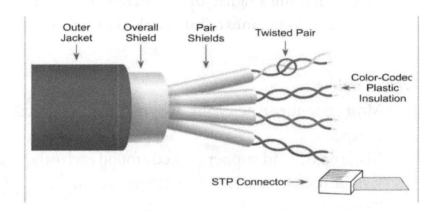

Fiber Optic Cable

- Fiber optic uses light to transmit data, instead of electrical signals.
- Light only moves in one direction – so, second connection is made between two devices for two way connection.
- Center of the fiber optic is glass strand.
- Light travels through this glass to other device

o Around core area, cladding of reflective material is there.
o So, light doesn't escape
o It supports bandwidth of more than 2 Gbps

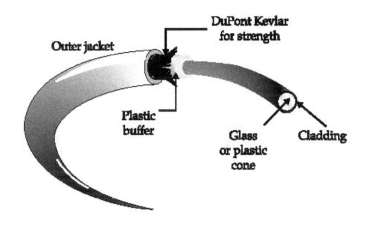

o No attenuation – no sensitivity to EMI
o Expensive to install
o Can be connected using following connectors:
  - LC
  - ST
  - SC
  - FC

Wireless Transmission Media
o Transmission is sent through the atmosphere.
o It can be used when physical obstruction or distance blocks the use of normal cable media.

Infrared

- o It is limited within 100 feet.
- o Within this range, however infrared is relatively fast.
- o Its high bandwidth supports transmission speed up to 10mbps.
- o Such devices are insensitive to radio frequency interference.
- o Four varieties:
  - o Broadband optical tele point
  - o Line of sight
  - o Reflective
  - o Scatter infrared

Laser Transmission

- o Laser transmission can transmit the data to very far distance.
- o But it is possible in line-of-sight communication.
- o The light emitted from a laser is monochromatic that is it is of one color / wavelength. (ordinary light is of many color)
- o Laser light is highly directional. (Ordinary light is emitted in many directions).

Radio Transmission

- o Radio wave transmission can be divided into two categories
- o Frequency hopping

- o It hops among several available frequencies
- o Stays on each frequency for a specified interval of time
- o Range of this type of transmissions is up to two miles
- o 250 kbps to 2 mbps
- Direct sequence modulation
  - o It breaks original messages into parts called chips which are transmitted on separate frequencies.
  - o Direct sequence modulation systems operates at 900 mhz and supports bandwidths of 2-6 mbps

Microwave

- Microwave technology is applicable in
  - o Wireless LAN
  - o Wireless extended LAN
  - o Mobile networking
- It can be done in two forms:
  - o Terrestrial (ground) links
  - o Satellite links
1. Terrestrial Microwave
   - o It implements earth-based transmitters and receivers.
   - o It operates in the low-gigahertz range, typically at 4-6 GHz and 21-23 GHz.

- o Requires direct antennas be pointed at each other – line of sight
- o Relay towers – used as repeaters to extend the distance of the transmission.
- o E.g.: telephone relay tower
- o Capacity – extremely high
- o Attenuation – determined by frequency, power, antenna size
- o Properly designed system – not affected by attenuation – under rain and fog

2. Satellite Microwave
   - o It can use satellite about 50,000 km. above the earth
   - o Satellite dishes are used to send and receive the signals
   - o Extremely expensive
   - o Operates in low Giga hertz : 11 – 14 ghz.
   - o Useful in mobile communication

Bluetooth

- o Bluetooth is a specification for the use of low-power radio communications to link phones, computers and other network devices over short distances without wires.
- o Bluetooth can transmit up to 30 feet (10 meters).
- o Bluetooth devices generally communicate at less than 1 Mbps.

- o Bluetooth networks feature a dynamic topology called a *piconet*.
- o Piconets contain a minimum of two and a maximum of eight Bluetooth peer devices.
- o It is useful to establish PAN (Personal Area Network)

- **Versions of BT**

1.1	Simply transfers the data from one device to another connected device
1.2	Less interference with other radio frequencies
2.0	Enhanced data rate
2.1	Secure Simple Pairing
3.0	The main new feature is high speed transport i.e. 24 mbits/sec
4.0	Bluetooth smart
5.0	Emerging Internet Of Things

Multiplexing and Switching concepts

Electromagnetic spectrum

CLASS	FREQUENCY
Y	300 EHz
	30 EHz
HX	3 EHz
	300 PHz
SX	30 PHz
EUV	3 PHz
NUV	
NIR	300 THz
MIR	30 THz
FIR	3 THz
	300 GHz
EHF	30 GHz
SHF	3 GHz
UHF	300 MHz
VHF	30 MHz
HF	3 MHz
MF	300 kHz
LF	30 kHz
VLF	3 kHz
VF/ULF	300 Hz
SLF	30 Hz
ELF	3 Hz

Multiplexing
- o It allows broadband media to support multiple channels.
- o It means it combines multiple data channels for transmission on a common medium.
- o Multiplexing and de - multiplexing are performed by a multiplexor (mux) which usually has both capabilities.

Frequency – Division Multiplexing (FDM)
- o Converts all data channels to analog form.
- o Each analog signal can be modulated by a separate frequency.
- o It supports bidirectional signaling on the same cable and useful for broadband LANs.

Time – Division Multiplexing (TDM)
- o It divides the channel in time slots that are allocated to the data streams to be transmitted.
- o If the channel is not busy then its time slot isn't being fully utilized.

Code Division Multiplexing (CDM)
- o Code division multiplexing (CDM) is a networking technique in which multiple data signals are combined for simultaneous transmission over a common frequency band.

o When CDM is used to allow multiple users to share a single communications channel, the technology is called **Code Division Multiple Access (CDMA).**

Wavelength Division Multiplexing (WDM)

o Wavelength-division multiplexing (WDM) is a method of combining multiple signals on laser beams at various infrared (IR) wavelengths for transmission along fiber optic media.

o Each laser is modulated by an independent set of signals. Wavelength-sensitive filters, the IR analog of visible-light color filters, are used at the receiving end.

o WDM is similar to frequency-division multiplexing (FDM). But instead of taking place at radio frequencies (RF), WDM is done in the IR portion of the electromagnetic spectrum.

o Each IR channel carries several RF signals combined by means of FDM or time-division multiplexing (TDM).

o Each multiplexed IR channel is separated, or de-multiplexed, into the original signals at the destination.

o Using FDM or TDM in each IR channel in combination with WDM or several IR channels, data in different formats and at different speeds can be transmitted simultaneously on a single fiber.

Switching Techniques

- o How the packets are switched from source to destination
- o Three types of switching techniques:

1. Circuit switching
   - o In circuit switching, a connection is established between two network nodes before they begin transmitting data.
   - o Bandwidth is dedicated to this connection and remains available until the users terminate communication between the two nodes.
   - o While the nodes remain connected, all data follows the same path initially selected by the switch.

2. Message switching
   - o A store – and – forward network where a complete message is transferred.

3. Packet switching
   - o Data is divided into packets and each packet has source / destination address information.
   - o Each packet may travel on different route.

Network Devices

LAN Card

- o It is also known as Network Interface Card (NIC).
- o It is a hardware component which is required to connect a computer to a network.
- o It is a device that enables computer to communicate over a network.
- o As it is a physical device, it provides access to a networking medium.
- o It also provides addressing system with the use of MAC.
- o So…It works in physical layer and data link layer.

Modem

- o It is derived from the terms **Modulation/Demodulation**.
- o Modulation means converting a signal from one form to another.
- o Demodulation means again convert the same signal to its original form.
- o Modems are classified in two categories:
    - o Asynchronous modems
    - o Synchronous modems
- • **DSL Modem**
    - o It stands for **Digital Subscriber Line (DSL)** modem.

- It is a device used to connect a computer to a telephone line which provides the digital subscriber line service for connectivity to the Internet.

- **ADSL Modem**
  - It stands for **Asymmetric DSL.**
  - The "asymmetric" means that more of the bandwidth of the line is dedicated to downstream (download) data than upstream (upload) data.
  - So, download rates are faster than upload rates.

Hub

- It is a central attachment point for network cabling.
- LAN established with coaxial cable doesn't use hubs.
- It comes in three types:
  - Active hub
  - Passive hub
  - Intelligent (Smart) hub

- **Active hubs**
  - It can amplify and clean up the electronic signals.
  - Cleaning up the signals is also called signal regeneration.
  - The network becomes less sensitive to errors.
  - Distance between devices can be increased.

- It can be said that active hubs also work as repeaters.

- **Passive hubs**
  - It does not contain any electronic components.
  - So, it does not process the signals in any way.
  - It only serves one purpose and i.e. to combine the signals from several network members.
  - As it does not amplify the signal, the length cannot be extended and distance between a system and a hub can be half of the maximum network distance.

- **Intelligent (Smart) hubs**
  - Intelligent hubs are improved active hubs.

- **Hub management:**
  - A network administrator can order the hub to shut down a connection that is generating network errors.

Repeaters
- It repeats the signal from one to other device
- It works at physical layer.
- It does not process the signal by any means. It simply repeats (regenerates) the signal in all directions.
- So, it does not require any addressing information.

o Using repeater, length of network can be extended.

Switch

o It is known as switching hubs.
o It routes the signals between ports and hub very quickly.
o It repeats a packet only to the port that connects to the destination computer.
o Many switching hubs have capability to choose the fastest path for packet.
o Available in two types:
  o Manageable
  o Non manageable

Bridges

o Bridges are used to extend the size of network.

Types of Bridges:
o Learning Bridge: Automatic updates address table
o Source Routing Bridge: Used in Token ring network
o Translation Bridge: Connects networks with different architecture
o Remote Bridge: Connects a LAN segment to other LAN segment

Routers

- o Organizes the large network in terms of logical network segment
- o Each segment is assigned an address
- o So every packet has:
  - o destination network address
  - o Destination device address
- o They build tables of network locations and also use algorithm to determine the most efficient path
- o Routers can be used to connect different network types.

Types of routers

1. Static Routers
2. Dynamic Routers

Routing algorithms

- o To decide the best path, router can use routing algorithms.
- o Route tables do not store only path information but also store estimates of time taken to send a message through a given route.
- o The time estimate is known as the cost of a particular path.

Methods for estimating routing costs

1. Hop count:

- Number of routers that a message might cross

2. Tic count

- Tic is a time unit
- It provides actual time estimate

Route selection

- **Static route selection:**
  - Routes are programmed by network administrator
- **Dynamic route selection:**
  - Uses routing cost information
  - If network conditions change then will be reflected in routing tables

- **Methods of routing**
  1. Distance Vector Routing
     - Advertise their presence periodically
     - Other routers can use the information
     - Takes time as all routers update the information
     - Increases network traffic
  2. Link – State Routing
     - Newly attached routers can request for information

o If any changes occur, then it will be broadcasted

o No need of complete network routing updates

Brouters

o It also works as Bridge
o It will deliver the packets based on network protocol information

Gateway

o It works at the Application layer
o It enables communication between dissimilar protocols system.
o It removes the layered protocol information of incoming packets and replace with necessary information

Wireless network devices

o Wireless switch
o Wireless router
o Access points

Access Point

o Wireless **access points** (APs or WAPs) are specially configured devices on wireless local area networks (WLANs).

- Access points act as a central transmitter and receiver of wireless radio signals including Wi-Fi.
- APs are most commonly used to support public Internet hotspots and also on internal business networks to extend their Wi-Fi signal range.

Packets

- o While data is divided into smaller groups, it results in smoother performance.
- o As the small packets don't engage transmission media for a long time, it becomes more efficient.
- o Packets are supporting in error detection and correction.
- o If error is detected then only that packet is to be retransmitted and that becomes the advantage.

Header

- o It specifies the start of packet and also contains various parameters like source and destination address.
- o Header also contains synchronization information.

Data

- o This portion contains actual data.

Trailer

- o It marks the end of the packet and generally contains error – checking like CRC information

Protocols

- Protocols are the rules by which computers communicate.
- Protocol suite or protocol stack have many protocols with different capabilities.
- Protocols are implemented at every stage like at the time of forming packets, transmitting them and again reform to original message at destination end.

TCP/IP Suite

- It is also referred as a DOD model as originally developed by United States – Department Of Defense (DOD).

IP (Internet Protocols)

- IP is the host – to – host network layer delivery protocol for internet.
- IP is unreliable and connectionless datagram protocol.
- IP provides no flow control.
- It uses only an error detection mechanism. So, it discards the packets if it is corrupted.
- IP does its best to deliver a packet to destination with no guarantees.

TCP (Transmission Control Protocol)

- o IP is to be paired with TCP if reliability is significant.
- o TCP is an inter network connection oriented protocol. It provides full duplex, end – to – end connections.
- o It opens and maintains connection between two hosts.
- o A TCP header adds flow control, sequencing, error checking.
- o TCP is not fast as UDP in terms of number of acknowledgement received.

Network Access Layer

- o This layer is responsible for placing and receiving TCP/IP packets on the network medium.
- o It can be used to connect different network types including Ethernet, Token Ring and WAN technologies etc.

Internet layer

- o This layer handles the transfer of data across multiple networks through the use of gateways and routers.
- o It provides a single service that is best effort connection less packet transfer.
- o IP packets (called datagrams) routed independently on different paths.

Host to Host Layer

- o It is designed to allow peer entities on the source and destination hosts to carry on conversation.
- o TCP works on this layer.
- o TCP is a reliable connection oriented protocol.

Application Layer

- o This layer does the same job as it is done by upper three layers of the OSI.
- o It contains all higher level protocol such as FTP, SMTP, NFS, HTTP

UDP (User Datagram Protocol)

- o It is a connection less, unreliable transport layer protocol.
- o It simply transport datagram and does not provide message acknowledgements.
- o It does not establish, maintain or control data flow.
- o It uses port numbers to deliver datagram.
- o UDP can be preferred than TCP because of low network overhead.

ARP (Address Resolution Protocol)

- o ARP maps and associates an IP address to a MAC address.

- On a LAN each device on a link identified by a physical address.
- A host/router needs to find MAC address of another one on network, it sends an ARP request.
- Packet includes physical & IP address of the sender and IP of the receiver. It does not know the physical address of the receiver and the query is broadcasted over the network.
- Every host/router receives & processes the ARP query packet and only intended recipient recognizes its IP address and sends back an ARP response packet.

ICMP

- It stands for Internet Control Message Protocol
- It provides error reporting for IP.
- It is a network layer protocol.
- Messages are not directly passed to the data link layer instead they are encapsulated inside IP datagram.
- If device cannot forward IP packet to the next network during its journey, it sends request to the source to send the message using ICMP.

FTP

- It stands for File Transfer Protocol

- o FTP is file sharing protocol used in TCP/IP environment
- o FTP allows users to remotely log on to other computers on a network, browse, download & upload files.
- o FTP is very popular, platform independent.
- o All kind of FTP servers & clients available for every operating system.

SMTP

- o It stands for Simple Mail Transfer Protocol
- o SMTP is responsible for making sure that email is delivered.
- o It only handles delivery of mail to servers and between servers.
- o It does not handle delivery to the final e-mail client application like creation, management, delivery of message performed by email applications.
- o It uses TCP and IP protocols.

TELNET

- o It means Remote Terminal Emulation
- o TELNET allows user to remotely log into another computer and run applications.
- o Computer on which the user physically working is dumb terminal, no processing is done on that computer.

o TELNET implements availability for end users.

Domain Name System
- o DNS system converts user friendly name to correct IP address.
- o To resolve the address, client first contact to main DNS server.
- o Here the client is guided to which server it has to contact.
- o Then client goes to proper server to resolve the full name of an IP and then main server point a client to closer server.

Network File System
- o It is developed by Sun Microsystems.
- o It is more advanced way to share files and disk drives than FTP and TELNET.
- o NFS allows users to get connected to network devices and use them as if they were local hard drives.
- o NFS specifications are available for public use.

IPX / SPX
- o They are netware protocols.
- o They are designed for high degree of modularity.

- Modularity makes Netware protocols adaptable to different hardware.
- They use two distinct addresses: host address & the network address
- Host address is based on the hardware address and network address is logical address assigned by the administrator.
- Addresses in an IPX/SPX network is represented as:
  - Host address : Network Address

IPX

- It stands for Internetwork Packet Exchange Protocol.
- It is a connectionless network layer protocol.
- It uses the RIP to make route selections.
- It depends on physical address that is found at lower layers to provide network device addressing.

SPX

- It stands for Sequenced Packet Exchange.
- It is a transport layer protocol.
- It extends IPX to provide connection oriented reliable delivery.
- Reliable delivery ensures retransmission of packets if any error occurs.
- It establishes virtual circuits (connections).
- SPX header comes with connection ID.

- When reliable transmission is needed, SPX is to be used.
- It immediately detects missing or damaged packets and it also sequences the packets.
- It also offers connection multiplexing.

Apple Talk
- It is a local area network communication protocol.
- It is developed by Apple computer for Macintosh family of personal computers.
- It is a computing architecture.
- First it was supporting Apple's proprietary localtalk system but then it was extended to incorporate Ethernet and physical layer.

DLC
- It stands for Data Link Control protocol.
- It is not a fully functioning protocol.
- It provides connectivity with IBM mainframes also.
- Every network interface card (NIC) has a DLC address or DLC identifier (DLCI) that uniquely identifies the node on the network.
- Protocols, such as TCP/IP, use a logical address at the Network Layer to identify nodes.
- Ultimately, however, all network addresses must be translated to DLC addresses.

o In TCP/IP networks, this translation is performed with the Address Resolution Protocol (ARP).

SMB

o SMB is the abbreviation of Server Message Block.
o It provides shared access to the resources.
o It also supports communications between nodes on a network.
o It provides authenticated inter – process communication mechanism.

NetBIOS Names

o It stands for Network Basic Input Output System.
o It works at Session layer.
o It allows applications of different computers to communicate over a local network.
o Unique computer name is called NetBIOS name.
o It works with TCP/IP so each computer in the network has IP address and a NetBIOS name.
o NetBIOS name can be 15 characters long.
o The name can be specified when Windows network is installed or configured.

L2CAP

o It stands for Logical Link Control and Adaption Protocol.
o It resides in the data link layer.

- It provides services to upper layer protocols.
- It supports protocol multiplexing capability and segmentation and reassembly operation.
- It permits one way transmission management of data to a group of other Bluetooth devices.

RFCOMM

- It is abbreviation of Radio Frequency COMMunication protocol.
- It is a transport protocol.
- It allows up to sixty simultaneous connections between Bluetooth devices.
- It provides simple reliable data stream to the user, like TCP.

SDP

- It is Service Discovery Protocol.
- It helps the systems to discover the available services and parameters required to be connected.
- It can be used in Bluetooth environment.
- Each service is identified by a UUID (Universally Unique Identifier).

CARP

- It stands for Common Address Redundancy Protocol.

o It allows multiple nodes of the same network (local) to share a set of IP addresses.

o It supports to provide failover redundancy especially when used with firewalls and routers.

o It may provide load balancing facility in some configurations.

Network Routing Protocol

It is used to specify the following:

o How routers communicate with each other,

o Broadcasting information that enables them to select routes,

o The selection of route being done by routing algorithms.

o Every router has knowledge of only network that is attached to it directly.

o First this information is shared with immediate neighbors and then throughout the network.

IP Addressing

Introduction

- o IP stands for Internet Protocol. It is a protocol that works at 3rd layer of OSI i.e. network layer.
- o It routes the packets between two nodes.
- o To meet this requirement, IP defines an addressing scheme.
- o An IP address is composed of 32 bits.
- o These 32 bits are further divided into 4 octets.
  - o For e.g. 172.65.10.24
- o Each octet is of 8 bits.
- o Computer understands these numbers in binary format only.
- o IP addresses are assigned to organizations in blocks.
- o Each block belongs to one of the classes.
- o By looking at the IP address, we can identify the class of it.
- o It is indicated in first octet of IP address.
- o When a class A IP license is granted, only the first octet is assigned.
- o The value of second, third and fourth octet can be assigned by the organization.
- o The default subnet mask for a class A network is 255.0.0.0.
- o There are 24 bits in these three octets.

Classes	1st byte	No. of addresses	Left most bits
Class A	1 – 127	2^{31}	0
Class B	128 – 191	2^{30}	10
Class C	192 – 223	2^{29}	110
Class D	224 – 239	2^{28}	1110
Class E	240 – 255	2^{28}	1111

- Each bit can be in one of the two states.
- So, 2^24 is the number of host addresses that can be assigned on that network.
- Two addresses are reserved on every network.
- So, maximum possible addresses are 2^24 – 2 that means 16,777,214.
- When class B is granted, first two octets are assigned.
- The default subnet mask for class B is 255.255.0.0
- 16 bits for host address field.

- Possible addresses -> $2^{16} - 2 = 65{,}534$
- When class C is granted, the first three octets are assigned.
- The default subnet mask for a class C is 255.255.255.0
- So, possible host addresses are $2^8 - 2 = 254$.
- Class D and class E are reserved for multicasting and research respectively.

Why Subnetting?

- In class A we can assign 16,777,214 nodes.
- But it may not be preferred by the organization to make one network of 16,777,214 nodes.
- The organization may want the nodes to be connected via small networks so they would divide huge network into subnetworks of nodes that communicate with each other frequently.
- This is called subnetting.
- It is a logical division.

Translating Binary to Decimal

E.g.: -
1 1 1 1 1 1 1 1
128 64 32 16 8 4 2 1
128+64+32+16+8+4+2+1 = 255

E.g.

1 0 1 1 1 0 0 1

   128   64 32 16 8 4 2 1

$128 + 0 + 32 + 16 + 8 + 0 + 0 + 1 = 185$

Converting Decimal to Binary

E.g.

   175   1 0 1 0 1 1 1 1

$128 + 0 + 32 + 0 + 8 + 4 + 2 + 1 = 175$

Subnetting

- Suppose in class B, network is 172.60.0.0 and subnet mask is 255.255.255.0 (after making third octet with all bits high).
- Here $2^8 - 2 = 254$ host address possible.
- But we may don't want 256/254 subnets on our class B network.
- We may use 255.255.224.0 as subnet mask.
- So, number of bits allocated is 3.
- Moreover, 8 bits of last octet are left. So, possible hosts on each subnet is $2^{13}-2 = 8190$.
- To know that the host is on which subnet, compare related octet.
- E.g. ➔ IP address = 172.60.50.2

Subnet mask = 255.255.224.0

50 = 00110010

224 = 11100000

Now perform AND operation and convert the result to binary.

Answer is 00100000 = 32

So, this host is on subnet 172.60.32.0

Supernet

- o A supernet is an Internet Protocol (IP) network that is formed from the combination of two or more networks or subnets.
- o In internet networking terminology, a supernet is a block of contiguous subnetworks addressed as a single subnet.

IPv6

- o It was developed by the Internet Engineering Task Force (IETF).
- o It is a internet layer protocol for packet – switched internetworking.
- o It provides end – to – end datagram transmission.
- o It uses 128 bit addresses (16 octets).
- o It can provide 3.403×10^{38} addresses.

Features

- o Multiple Header Structure

- o It simplifies aspects of address assignment, network renumbering and router announcements.
- o It has fixed the host identifies portion of an address to 64 bits.
- o Network security is also integrated into the design of the IPv6 architecture.

Windows 2008 server

Accounts
- o User
- o Group
- o Computers

User accounts
- o Administrator account
- o Guest account
- o Remote assistance

Account options
- o User must change password at next logon
- o User cannot change password
- o Password never expires
- o Account is disabled
- o Smart card is required
- o Account is trusted for delegation

Monitoring performance
- o Windows server 2003 includes both
  - o Task manager (for simple monitoring)
  - o System monitor (for powerful monitoring)
    - Memory
    - Physical disk

- Processor
- Network traffic management
  - Processor time
  - Physical disk % and disk time
  - Pages / sec in memory
  - Bytes sent / sec
  - Bytes received / sec
  - Total bytes / sec
  - Frames sent and received / sec
  - Segments sent and received / sec

How to optimize network performance?

- Unbind surplus devices
- Try to place all related users in one subnet
- Sequence and use of protocols

Logging events

- HKEY_LOCAL_MACHINE\SYSTEM \ CurrentControlSet\Services\NTDS\Diagnostics
  - Security events
    - such as a user who tries to read or write an attribute with insufficient permissions
  - Replication events
    - Events related to outbound replication, where changed objects are found and

inbound replication, where these changes are applied to a local database.

- o Garbage collection
  - Events generated when objects marked for deletion are actually deleted.
- o Directory access
  - Reads and writes directory objects from all sources.

Logging levels
- o 0 (None)
- o 1 (minimal)
- o 2 (Basic)
- o 3 (Extensive)
- o 4 (Verbose)
- o 5 (Internal)

Note: Configure every event with one of the levels

MMC
- o It stands for Microsoft Management Control
- o It comes as a component of Windows 2000 and its later versions.
- o It provides an interface for configuring and monitoring the system.
- o MMC 3.0 simplifies day-to-day system management tasks by providing GUI interface.
- o **MMC tools are called snap-ins.**

- It does not perform the functions, instead it hosts a variety of tools.
- Snap-ins are registered in the
  - HKEY_LOCAL_MACHINE\Software\Micr osoft\MMC\Snapins

Basics of Network Security

What is Network Security?

- o Network security consists of the provisions and policies adopted by a network administrator to prevent and monitor unauthorized access, misuse or modification of a computer network and network-accessible resources.
- o Network security involves the **authorization of access** to data in a network, which is controlled by the network administrator.
- o Users choose or are assigned an ID and password or other authenticating information that allows them access to information and programs within their authority.

Fundamental Questions for N/W Security

- o What are you trying to protect or maintain?
- o What are your business objectives?
- o What do you need to accomplish these objectives?
- o What technologies or solutions are required to support these objectives?
- o Are your objectives compatible with your security infrastructure, operations and tools?
- o What risks are associated with inadequate security?
- o What are the implications of not implementing security?

o Will you introduce new risks not covered by your current security solutions or policy?
o How do you reduce that risk?
o What is your tolerance for risk?

Security Methods
o Encryption
o Cryptography
o Authentication

Encryption

- Encryption is the conversion of data into a form, called a cipher text, which cannot be easily understood by unauthorized people.
- Simple ciphers include the substitution of letters for numbers
- More complex ciphers rearrange the letters.
- In order to easily recover the contents of an encrypted signal, the correct decryption key is required.

Cryptography

- Discipline or techniques employed in protecting integrity or secrecy of electronic messages by converting them into unreadable form.

- Only the use of a secret key can convert the cipher text back into human readable (clear text) form.
- Cryptography software and/or hardware devices use mathematical formulas (algorithms) to change text from one form to another.

Authentication

- Authentication is the process of determining the true identity of someone.
- Basic authentication is simply using a password to verify that you are who you say you are.
- Next level of authentication involves way other than password which can use biometric method to identify the authority.
    - For e.g. finger print matching, face detection, retina matching etc..

The CIA model

- o Confidentiality, Integrity and Availability

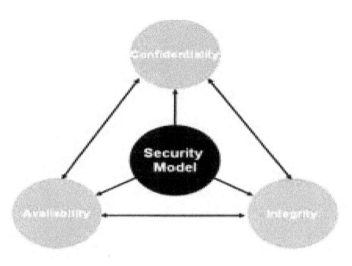

Confidentiality

- o It prevents unauthorized access of sensitive information.
- o It ensures that the information is hidden from unauthorized users.
- o Cryptography or encryption is such examples.

Integrity

- o It ensures unauthorized modification of data, systems or information.
- o It ensures unchanged representation of the original secure information.

Availability

- o It keeps the resources available for access.
- o It ensures that information needed by authorized users is readily available.

Security policies

- o Acceptable use
- o Ethics
- o Information sensitivity
- o E-mail
- o Password
- o Risk assessment

Security standards

- o Standards are best practices by industries.
- o ISO 17799 and COBIT
  - o COBIT stands for **C**ontrol **Ob**jectives for **I**nformation and related **T**echnology.
  - o It is a framework with guidance that focuses on "What needs to be achieved" rather than "How to achieve."

Security procedures, baselines and guidelines

- o Procedures are low-level documents which provides systematic instructions on how the policy and standards are implemented.
- o A baseline is the minimum level of security requirement in a system.

o Guidelines are suggested actions and operational guides for users.

Security wheel

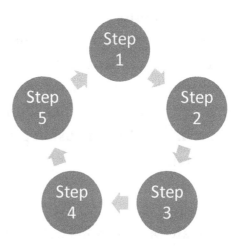

1. **Develop a security policy**
   o This is the step where we implement our security solutions in the enterprise.
   o Firewalls, authentication, encryption are included in this step. Questions that can be asked in this step may include:
   o What kind of firewalls do we want?
   o Where should we put the firewall?
   o Where and when should we use authentication? Use password, fingerprint or something else?

- o What type of encryption should we use? What kind of information that we should encrypt?

2. Make the network secure

3. Monitor and respond

- o This is the step where we monitor our security solutions implemented in the previous step.
- o We should monitor if a security breach exists.
- o We can think about IDS (***Intrusion detection system***) or IPS (***Intrusion prevention system***) in this stage.
- o This step can be used to validate our security solutions.
- o How are our solutions defending the enterprise's network? Good, bad, need improvement?

4. Test

- o This is the step where the security engineers/specialists try to break their own security solutions.

5. Manage and improve

- o Once we find a breach or something that hinders employee's productivity, then we can improve it here. This may also be a good place to change our security policy.

o Confidentiality, integrity and availability, also
known as the CIA triad, is a model designed to
guide policies for information security within an
organization.

o The model is also sometimes referred to as the
AIC triad (availability, integrity and
confidentiality) to avoid confusion with the
Central Intelligence Agency. The elements of the
triad are considered the three most crucial
components of security.

Confidentiality:

o Confidentiality is roughly equivalent to privacy.
Measures undertaken to ensure confidentiality are
designed to prevent sensitive information from
reaching the wrong people, while making sure that
the right people can in fact get it: Access must be
restricted to those authorized to view the data in
question.

o It is common, as well, for data to be categorized
according to the amount and type of damage that
could be done should it fall into unintended hands.

More or less stringent measures can then be implemented according to those categories.

Integrity:
- o Integrity involves maintaining the consistency, accuracy, and trustworthiness of data over its entire life cycle. Data must not be changed in transit, and steps must be taken to ensure that data cannot be altered by unauthorized people (for example, in a breach of confidentiality).
- o These measures include file permissions and user access controls. Version control maybe used to prevent erroneous changes or accidental deletion by authorized users becoming a problem. In addition, some means must be in place to detect any changes in data that might occur as a result of non-human-caused events such as an electromagnetic pulse (EMP) or server crash.
- o Some data might include checksums, even cryptographic checksums, for verification of integrity. Backups or redundancies must be available to restore the affected data to its correct state.

Availability:
- o Availability is best ensured by rigorously maintaining all hardware, performing hardware repairs immediately when needed and maintaining a

correctly functioning operating system environment that is free of software conflicts.

o It's also important to keep current with all necessary system upgrades. Providing adequate communication bandwidth and preventing the occurrence of bottlenecks are equally important.

o Redundancy, failover, RAID even high-availability clusters can mitigate serious consequences when hardware issues do occur. Fast and adaptive disaster recovery is essential for the worst-case scenarios; that capacity is reliant on the existence of a comprehensive disaster recovery plan (DRP). Safeguards against data loss or interruptions in connections must include unpredictable events such as natural disasters and fire.

o To prevent data loss from such occurrences, a backup copy may be stored in a geographically-isolated location, perhaps even in a fireproof, waterproof safe. Extra security equipment or software such as firewalls and proxy servers can guard against downtime and unreachable data due to malicious actions such as denial-of-service (DoS) attacks and network intrusions.

Non-repudiation:

o Non-repudiation is the presentation of unforgeable evidence that a message was sent or received. If messages or transactions can be disputed, then important identity actions can be challenged and jeopardized.

o These disputes can take two forms. Consider two people, Alice and Bob who are exchanging messages. In one case, Alice denies sending a message to Bob that he claims to have received. Being able to counter Alice's denial is called Non-Repudiation of Origin (NRO). In the second case, Alice claims to have sent

Security and Network Attacks

o It consists of the provisions and policies adopted by a network administrator to prevent and monitor unauthorized access, misuse, modification, or denial of a computer network and network-accessible resources. Network security involves the authorization of access to data in a network, which is controlled by the network administrator. Users choose or are assigned an ID and password or other authenticating information that allows them access to information and programs within their authority.

o Network security covers a variety of computer networks, both public and private, that are used in everyday jobs conducting transactions and communications among businesses, government agencies and individuals. Networks can be private, such as within a company, and others which might be open to public access. Network security is involved in organizations, enterprises, and other types of institutions. It does as its title explains: It secures the network, as well as protecting and overseeing operations being done. The most common and simple way of protecting a network resource is by assigning it a unique name and a corresponding password.

Types of Attacks?

o Networks are subject to attacks from malicious sources. Attacks can be from two categories: "Passive" when a network intruder intercepts data traveling through the network, and "Active" in which an intruder initiates commands to disrupt the network's normal operation

Types of attacks include:

❖ **Passive**
   o **Network**
      ▪ Wiretapping

- Port scanner
- Idle scan
  - **Active**
    - Denial-of-service attack
    - Spoofing
    - Man in the middle
    - ARP poisoning
    - Smurf attack
    - Buffer overflow
    - Heap overflow
    - Format string attack
    - SQL injection
    - Cyber attack

Wiretapping

- Telephone tapping (also wiretapping or wiretapping in American English) is the monitoring of telephone and Internet conversations by a third party, often by covert means. The wiretap received its name because, historically, the monitoring connection was an actual electrical tap on the telephone line. Legal wiretapping by a government agency is also called lawful interception. Passive wiretapping monitors or records the traffic, while active wiretapping alters or otherwise affects it.

Port Scanner

A port scanner is a software application designed to probe a server or host for open ports. This is often used by administrators to verify security policies of their networks and by attackers to identify running services on a host with the view to compromise it.

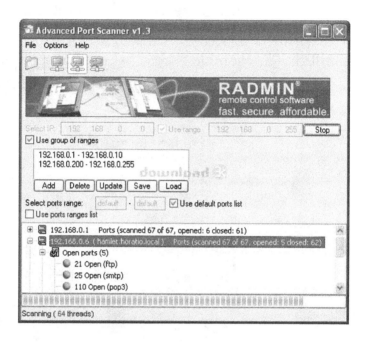

- o A port scan or portscan can be defined as a process that sends client requests to a range of server port addresses on a host, with the goal of finding an active port. While not a nefarious process in and of itself, it is one used by hackers to probe target machine services with the aim of exploiting a known vulnerability of that service. However the majority of uses of a port scan are not attacks and are simple probes to determine services available on a remote machine.

Idle Scan

o The idle scan is a TCP port scan method that consists of sending spoofed packets to a computer to find out what services are available. This is accomplished by impersonating another computer called a "zombie" (that is not transmitting or receiving information) and observing the behavior of the "zombie" system

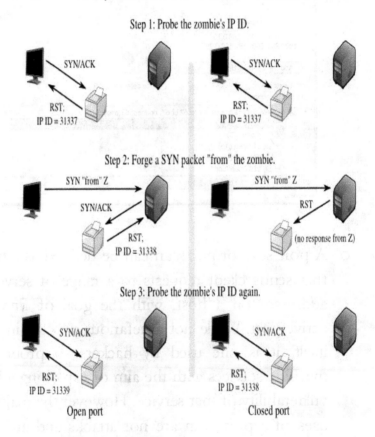

Step 1: Probe the zombie's IP ID.

SYN/ACK

RST;
IP ID = 31337

SYN/ACK

RST;
IP ID = 31337

Step 2: Forge a SYN packet "from" the zombie.

SYN "from" Z

SYN/ACK

RST;
IP ID = 31338

SYN "from" Z

RST

(no response from Z)

Step 3: Probe the zombie's IP ID again.

SYN/ACK

RST;
IP ID = 31339

Open port

SYN/ACK

RST;
IP ID = 31338

Closed port

Denial-of-Service Attack

o Denial-of-Service (DoS) or distributed denial-of-service (DDoS) attack is an attempt to make a machine or network resource unavailable to its intended users.

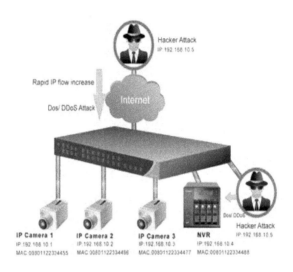

o Although the means to carry out, the motives for, and targets of a DoS attack vary, it generally consists of efforts to temporarily or indefinitely interrupt or suspend services of a host connected to the Internet.

ARP Poisoning

- ARP Spoofing/ Poisoning is a technique whereby an attacker sends fake ("spoofed") Address Resolution Protocol (ARP) messages onto a Local Area Network. Generally, the aim is to associate the attacker's MAC address with the IP address of another host (such as the default gateway), causing any traffic meant for that IP address to be sent to the attacker instead.
- ARP spoofing may allow an attacker to intercept data frames on a LAN, modify the traffic, or stop the traffic altogether. Often the attack is used as an opening for other attacks, such as denial of service, man in the middle, or session hijacking attacks.

ARP Spoofing

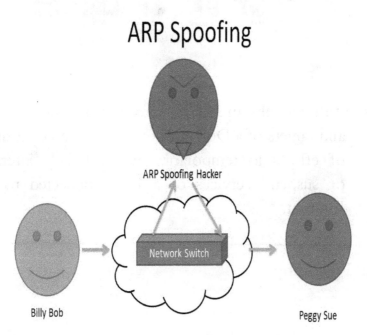

ARP Spoofing Hacker

Network Switch

Billy Bob

Peggy Sue

Smurf Attack

o The Smurf Attack is a distributed denial-of-service attack in which large numbers of Internet Control Message Protocol (ICMP) packets with the intended victim's spoofed source IP are broadcast to a computer network using an IP Broadcast address. Most devices on a network will, by default, respond to this by sending a reply to the source IP address.

o If the number of machines on the network that receive and respond to these packets is very large, the victim's computer will be flooded with traffic. This can slow down the victim's computer to the point where it becomes impossible to work on.

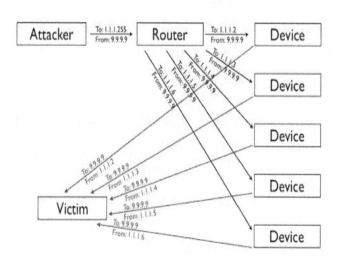

Buffer Overflow

o In computer security and programming, a buffer overflow, or buffer overrun, is an anomaly where a program, while writing data to a buffer, overruns the buffer's boundary and overwrites adjacent memory. This is a special case of violation of memory safety.

o Buffer overflows can be triggered by inputs that are designed to execute code, or alter the way the program operates. This may result in erratic program behavior, including memory access errors, incorrect results, a crash, or a breach of system security. Thus, they are the basis of many software vulnerabilities and can be maliciously exploited.

o Programming languages commonly associated with buffer overflows include C and C++, which provide no built-in protection against accessing or overwriting data in any part of memory and do not automatically check that data written to an array (the built-in buffer type) is within the boundaries of that array. Bounds checking can prevent buffer overflows.

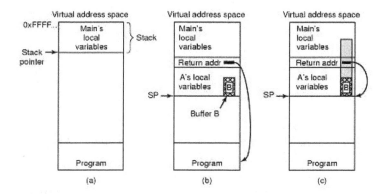

- (a) Situation when main program is running
- (b) After program *A* called
- (c) Buffer overflow shown in gray

Heap Overflow

- A heap overflow is a type of buffer overflow that occurs in the heap data area. Heap overflows are exploitable in a different manner to that of stack-based overflows. Memory on the heap is dynamically allocated by the application at run-time and typically contains program data.

- Exploitation is performed by corrupting this data in specific ways to cause the application to overwrite internal structures such as linked list pointers. The canonical heap overflow technique overwrites dynamic memory allocation linkage (such as malloc meta data) and uses the resulting pointer exchange to overwrite a program function pointer.

Format String Attack

- o Uncontrolled format string is a type of software vulnerability, discovered around 1999, that can be used in security exploits. Previously thought harmless, format string exploits can be used to crash a program or to execute harmful code.

- o The problem stems from the use of unchecked user input as the format string parameter in certain C functions that perform formatting, such as "printf()".A malicious user may use the "%s" & "%x" format tokens, among others, to print data from the stack or possibly other locations in memory.

- o One may also write arbitrary data to arbitrary locations using the "%n" format token, which commands "printf()"and similar functions to write the number of bytes formatted to an address stored on the stack.

Cyber Attack

- Cyber-attack is any type of offensive maneuver employed by individuals or whole organizations that targets computer information systems, infrastructures, computer networks, and/or personal computer devices by various means of malicious acts usually originating from an anonymous source that either steals, alters, or destroys a specified target by hacking into a susceptible system.

- These can be labelled as either a Cyber campaign, cyberwarfare or cyberterrorism in different context. Cyber-attacks can range from installing spyware on a PC to attempts to destroy the infrastructure of entire nations. Cyber - attacks have become increasingly sophisticated and dangerous as the Stuxnet worm recently demonstrated

Internet Connection and Sharing

Basics of Internet

- o In 1969, the US Department of Defense started a project to allow researchers and military personnel to communicate with each other in an emergency.
- o The project was called **ARPAnet** and it is the foundation of the **Internet**.
- o Concept of World Wide Web was introduced in 1990s.
- o The **Internet** is a global system of interconnected computer networks that use the standard Internet protocol suite (TCP/IP) to serve several billion users worldwide.
- o It is a network of networks that consists of millions of private, public, academic, business, and government networks, of local to global scope, that are linked by a broad array of electronic, wireless, and optical networking technologies.
- o All computers on the Internet can be lumped into two groups: servers and clients, which communicate with one another.
- o Independent computers connected to a server are called clients. Most likely, your home or office computer does not provide services to other computers. Therefore, it is a client.

o Your web browser (such as Internet Explorer or Netscape) is client software

Dial-up technology

o A Dial up Connection is a temporary, non-dedicated internet connection which is made by ordinary telephone lines through dialing an internet service provider's number.
o It is established by a modem which joins the computer to phone lines.
o When a user start a dial-up connection, the modem dials a phone number of an Internet Service Provider which then establishes the connection followed by several beeping and buzzing sounds.

ISDN Technology

o **Integrated Services Digital Network**
o **ISDN** is a network technology that supports digital transfer of simultaneous voice and data traffic.
o It works over ordinary telephone lines.
o Generally supports data rates of 128 Kbps.

Lease line technology

o A **leased line** connects two locations for private voice and/or data telecommunication service.

- o Leased line is actually a reserved circuit between two points.
- o They maintain a single open circuit at all times, as opposed to traditional telephone services that reuse the same lines for many different conversations through a process called "switching."
- o Leased lines most commonly are rented by businesses to connect branch offices, because these lines guarantee bandwidth for network traffic.

VPN

- o A virtual private network (VPN) is a network that uses a public telecommunication infrastructure, such as the Internet, to provide remote offices or individual users with secure access to their organization's network.
- o VPN follows a client and server approach. VPN clients authenticate users, encrypt data, and otherwise manage sessions with VPN servers utilizing a technique called **tunneling**.

Types of VPN
- o Remote access VPN
- o Intranet VPN
- o Extranet VPN

VPN Topology: Remote Access VPN

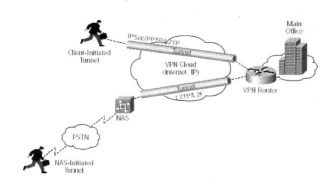

VPN Topology: Intranet VPN

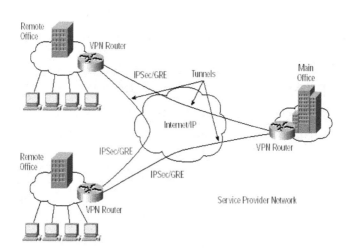

VPN Components: Protocols
- o IP Security (IPSec)
    - o Transport mode
    - o Tunnel mode
- o Point-to-Point Tunneling Protocol (PPTP)

- o Voluntary tunneling method
- o Uses PPP (Point-to-Point Protocol)
- o Layer 2 Tunneling Protocol (L2TP)
  - o Exists at the data link layer of OSI
- o Composed from PPTP and L2F (Layer 2 Forwarding)

Proxy server

- o In an enterprise that uses the Internet, a proxy server is a server that acts as an intermediary between a workstation user and the Internet so that the enterprise can ensure security, administrative control etc.
- o A proxy server is associated with or part of a gateway server that separates the enterprise network from the outside network.

Firewall

- A **network firewall** protects a computer network from unauthorized access.
- Network firewalls may be hardware devices, software programs, or a combination of the two.
- All messages entering or leaving the network pass through the firewall, which examines each message and blocks those that do not meet the specified security criteria.

GPS

- It stands for Global Positioning System (GPS).
- It is a satellite-based navigation system made up of a network of 24 satellites placed into orbit.
- GPS satellites circle the earth twice a day in a very precise orbit and transmit signal information to earth.
- GPS receivers take this information and use triangulation to calculate the user's exact location.
- A GPS receiver must be locked on to the signal of at least three satellites to calculate a 2D position (latitude and longitude).
- With four or more satellites in view, the receiver can determine the user's 3D position (latitude, longitude and altitude).
- Once the user's position has been determined, the GPS unit can calculate other information, such as

speed, bearing, track, trip distance, distance to destination, sunrise and sunset time and more.
- o The first GPS satellite was launched in 1978.
- o A full constellation of 24 satellites was achieved in 1994.
- o Each satellite is built to last about 10 years.
- o Replacements are constantly being built and launched into orbit.

GPRS
- o **General Packet Radio Service.**
- o It is a packet oriented mobile data service.
- o It supports IP and PPP.
- o The GPRS mobile phones can be classified into the following three classes in terms of the possibility of simultaneous calls (via GSM) and data transmission (via GPRS)...

  - Class A : Simultaneous calls (via GSM) and data transmission (via GPRS)

  - Class B : Automatic switching between the GSM and the GPRS mode is possible according to telephone settings.

  - Class C : Hand operated switching between the GSM and the GPRS mode

CCTV Technology

- o CCTV stands for closed-circuit television.
- o It is a TV system in which signals are not publicly distributed but are monitored, primarily for surveillance and security purposes.
- o CCTV relies on strategic placement of cameras.
- o Observation of the camera's input on monitors can be done for high security purpose.
- o Cameras can communicate via guided or unguided medium.
- o They are called closed circuit as the access to their content is limited to only few systems or people.
- o Modern CCTV displays color, high-resolution displays and can include the ability to zoom in on an image.
- o Talk CCTV allows an overseer to speak to people within range of the camera's associated speakers.
- o Recent advances in technology and software mean many advanced features such as Motion Recording.
- o When set to motion, record devices will only record when the CCTV camera detects motion. This saves storage space because the device is not recording during periods of inactivity.

Cryptography and Security

Basic of cryptography

- o Cryptography is the science of using mathematics to encrypt and decrypt data. Cryptography enables you to store sensitive information or transmit it across insecure networks (like the Internet) so that it cannot be read by anyone except the intended recipient.

- o While cryptography is the science of securing data, cryptanalysis is the science of analyzing and breaking secure communication. Classical cryptanalysis involves an interesting combination of analytical reasoning, application of mathematical tools, pattern finding, patience, determination, and luck. Cryptanalysts are also called attackers.

Basic Terminology

- o Sender: who sends the information?
- o Receiver: who accept the information comes from sender

- o Plain text: our information.
- o Cipher text: the text which is been encrypted.

Encryption and decryption

- o Data that can be read and understood without any special measures is called plaintext or clear text. The method of disguising plaintext in such a way as to hide its substance is called encryption.

- o Encrypting plaintext results in unreadable gibberish called cipher text. You use encryption to make sure that information is hidden from anyone for whom it is not intended, even those who can see the encrypted data. The process of reverting cipher text to its original plaintext is called decryption.

Requirement of Cryptography
We need cryptography for many reason:

- o Whenever we are transferring any important information at that time it is necessary that our information must transfer safely
- o To protect our data from hackers
- o To protect our data that it cannot reaches the receiver as half text or corrupted text.

- So with the help of the cryptography technique we can encrypt our data so that no can read that data except sender and receiver.

Types of Cryptography

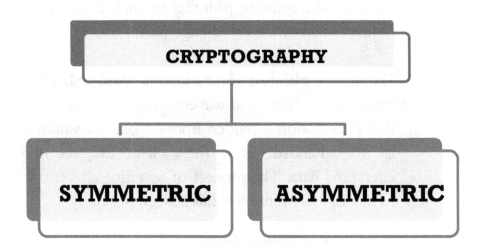

Symmetric key cryptography

- In symmetric key cryptography, the same key is used by both parties. The sender uses same key as to encrypt the data and receiver uses same key to decrypt the data. Symmetric key cryptography is useful if you want to encrypt files on your computer, and you intend to decrypt them yourself.

- It is less useful if you intend to send them to someone else to be decrypted, because in that case you have a "key distribution problem": securely communicating the encryption key to your correspondent may not be much easier than securely communicating the original text.

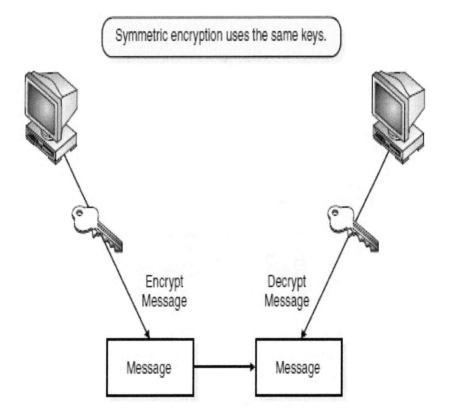

Symmetric Key algorithm

- The symmetric key algorithm are as follows:
- Caesar cipher

- o Data Encryption Standard (DES)
- o Block and stream cipher

Caesar cipher

- o The Caesar Cipher, also known as a shift cipher, is one of the oldest and simplest forms of encrypting a message. It is a type of substitution cipher where each letter in the original message (which in cryptography is called the plaintext) is replaced with a letter corresponding to a certain number of letters shifted up or down in the alphabet.
- o For each letter of the alphabet, you would take its position in the alphabet, say 3 for the letter 'C', and shift it by the key number. If we had a key of +3, that 'C' would be shifted down to an 'F' - and that same process would be applied to every letter in the plaintext.

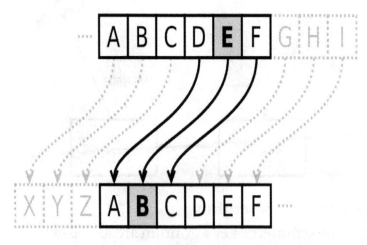

Data Encryption Standard (DES)

- o The Data Encryption Standard (DES) is a symmetric-key block cipher published by the National Institute of Standards and Technology (NIST).

- o DES is an implementation of a Feistel Cipher. It uses 16 round Feistel structure. The block size is 64-bit. Though, key length is 64-bit, DES has an effective key length of 56 bits, since 8 of the 64 bits of the key are not used by the encryption algorithm (function as check bits only).

Block Ciphers

- o In this scheme, the plain binary text is processed in blocks (groups) of bits at a time; i.e. a block of plaintext bits is selected, a series of operations is performed on this block to generate a block of cipher text bits.

- o The number of bits in a block is fixed. For example, the schemes DES and AES have block sizes of 64 and 128, respectively.

Stream Ciphers

- o In this scheme, the plaintext is processed one bit at a time i.e. one bit of plaintext is taken, and a series of operations is performed on it to generate one bit of ciphertext. Technically, stream ciphers are block ciphers with a block size of one bit.

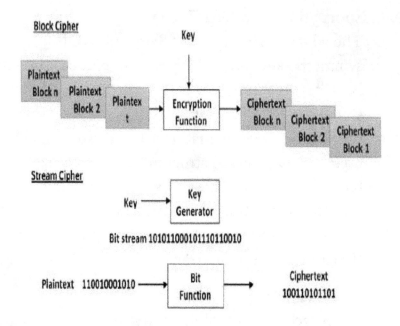

Asymmetric key cryptography

o Asymmetric cryptography, also known as public key cryptography, uses public and private keys to encrypt and decrypt data. The keys are simply large numbers that have been paired together but are not identical (asymmetric).

o One key in the pair can be shared with everyone; it is called the public key. The other key in the pair is kept secret; it is called the private key. Either of the keys can be used to encrypt a message; the opposite key from the one used to encrypt the message is used for decryption.

o The most important properties of public key encryption scheme are –

o Different keys are used for encryption and decryption. This is a property which set this scheme different than symmetric encryption scheme.

o Each receiver possesses a unique decryption key, generally referred to as his private key.

o Receiver needs to publish an encryption key, referred to as his public key.

o Some assurance of the authenticity of a public key is needed in this scheme to avoid spoofing by adversary as the receiver. Generally, this type of cryptosystem involves trusted third party which certifies that a particular public key belongs to a specific person or entity only.

o Encryption algorithm is complex enough to prohibit attacker from deducing the plaintext from the cipher text and the encryption (public) key.

o Though private and public keys are related mathematically, it is not be feasible to calculate the private key from the public key. In fact, intelligent part of any public-key cryptosystem is in designing a relationship between two keys.

Asymmetric Key algorithm

- o The Asymmetric key algorithm are as follows:
- o RSA
- o Diffe Hellman
- o DSS

RSA Algorithm

- o RSA algorithm is asymmetric cryptography algorithm. Asymmetric actually means that it works on two different keys i.e. **Public Key** and **Private Key.** As the name describes that the Public Key is given to everyone and Private key is kept private.
- o The idea of RSA is based on the fact that it is difficult to factorize a large integer. The public key consists of two numbers where one number is multiplication of two large prime numbers. And private key is also derived from the same two prime numbers. So if somebody can factorize the large number, the private key is compromised.
- o Therefore encryption strength totally lies on the key size and if we double or triple the key size, the strength of encryption increases exponentially. RSA keys can be typically 1024 or 2048 bits long, but experts believe that 1024 bit keys could be broken in

the near future. But till now it seems to be an infeasible task.

Diffe Hellman Algorithm

o The Diffie-Hellman algorithm is being used to establish a shared secret that can be used for secret communications while exchanging data over a public network using the elliptic curve to generate points and get the secret key using the parameters.

o For the sake of simplicity and practical implementation of the algorithm, we will consider only 4 variables one prime P and G (a primitive root of P) and two private values a and b.

o P and G are both publicly available numbers. Users (say Alice and Bob) pick private values a and b and they generate a key and exchange it publicly, the opposite person received the key and from that generates a secret key after which they have the same secret key to encrypt

DSS Algorithm

o Digital Signature Standard (DSS) is the digital signature algorithm (DSA) developed by the U.S. National Security Agency (NSA) to generate a digital signature for the authentication of electronic documents.

- DSS was put forth by the National Institute of Standards and Technology (NIST) in 1994, and has become the United States government standard for authentication of electronic documents. DSS is specified in Federal Information Processing Standard (FIPS) 186.
- DSA is a pair of large numbers that are computed according to the specified algorithm within parameters that enable the authentication of the signatory, and as a consequence, the integrity of the data attached. Digital signatures are generated through DSA, as well as verified. Signatures are generated in conjunction with the use of a private key; verification takes place in reference to a corresponding public key.
- Each signatory has their own paired public (assumed to be known to the general public) and private (known only to the user) keys. Because a signature can only be generated by an authorized person using their private key, the corresponding public key can be used by anyone to verify the signature.

Public Key Management (PKI)

- The most distinct feature of Public Key Infrastructure (PKI) is that it uses a pair of keys to achieve the underlying security service. The key pair comprises of private key and public key.

o Since the public keys are in open domain, they are likely to be abused. It is, thus, necessary to establish and maintain some kind of trusted infrastructure to manage these keys.

Key Management

o It goes without saying that the security of any cryptosystem depends upon how securely its keys are managed. Without secure procedures for the handling of cryptographic keys, the benefits of the use of strong cryptographic schemes are potentially lost.

o It is observed that cryptographic schemes are rarely compromised through weaknesses in their design. However, they are often compromised through poor key management.

o There are some important aspects of key management which are as follows −

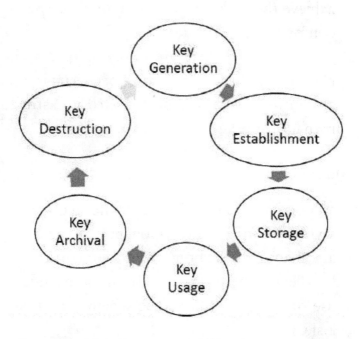

o Cryptographic keys are nothing but special pieces of data. Key management refers to the secure administration of cryptographic keys.

o Key management deals with entire key lifecycle as depicted in the following illustration

o There are two specific requirements of key management for public key cryptography.

o Secrecy of private keys. Throughout the key lifecycle, secret keys must remain secret from all parties except those who are owner and are authorized to use them.

o Assurance of public keys. In public key cryptography, the public keys are in open domain and seen as public pieces of data. By default there are no assurances of whether a public key is correct, with whom it can be associated, or what it can be used for. Thus key management of public keys needs to focus much more explicitly on assurance of purpose of public keys.

o The most crucial requirement of 'assurance of public key' can be achieved through the public-key infrastructure (PKI), a key management system for supporting public-key cryptography.

Public Key Infrastructure (PKI)

PKI provides assurance of public key. It provides the identification of public keys and their distribution. An anatomy of PKI comprises of the following components.

- Public Key Certificate, commonly referred to as 'digital certificate'.

- Private Key tokens.

- Certification Authority.

- Registration Authority.

- Certificate Management System.

Digital Certificate

- o For analogy, a certificate can be considered as the ID card issued to the person. People use ID cards such as a driver's license, passport to prove their identity. A digital certificate does the same basic thing in the electronic world, but with one difference.

- o Digital Certificates are not only issued to people but they can be issued to computers, software packages or anything else that need to prove the identity in the electronic world.

- o Digital certificates are based on the ITU standard X.509 which defines a standard certificate format for public key certificates and certification validation. Hence digital certificates are sometimes also referred to as X.509 certificates.

- o Public key pertaining to the user client is stored in digital certificates by The Certification Authority (CA) along with other relevant information such as client information, expiration date, usage, issuer etc.

- o CA digitally signs this entire information and includes digital signature in the certificate.

- o Anyone who needs the assurance about the public key and associated information of client, he carries out the signature validation process using CA's public key. Successful validation assures that the public key given in the certificate belongs to the person whose details are given in the certificate.

- o The process of obtaining Digital Certificate by a person/entity is depicted in the following illustration.

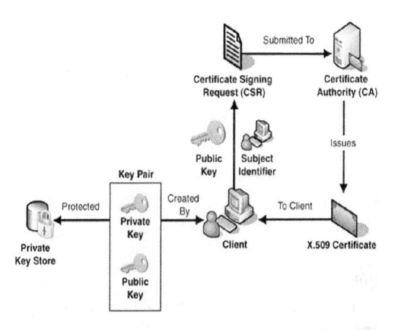

- o As shown in the illustration, the CA accepts the application from a client to certify his public key. The CA, after duly verifying identity of client, issues a digital certificate to that client.

Certifying Authority (CA)

- o As discussed above, the CA issues certificate to a client and assist other users to verify the certificate. The CA takes responsibility for identifying correctly the identity of the client asking for a certificate to be issued and ensures that the information contained within the certificate is correct and digitally signs it.

Key Functions of CA

The key functions of a CA are as follows —

- **Generating key pairs** — The CA may generate a key pair independently or jointly with the client.

- **Issuing digital certificates** — The CA could be thought of as the PKI equivalent of a passport agency — the CA issues a certificate after client provides the credentials to confirm his identity. The CA then signs the certificate to prevent modification of the details contained in the certificate.

- **Publishing Certificates** — The CA need to publish certificates so that users can find them. There are two ways of achieving this. One is to publish certificates in the equivalent of an electronic telephone directory. The other is to send your certificate out to those people you think might need it by one means or another.

- **Verifying Certificates** — The CA makes its public key available in environment to assist verification of his signature on clients' digital certificate.

- **Revocation of Certificates** – At times, CA revokes the certificate issued due to some reason such as compromise of private key by user or loss of trust in the client. After revocation, CA maintains the list of all revoked certificate that is available to the environment.

Classes of Certificates

There are four typical classes of certificate –

- **Class 1** – These certificates can be easily acquired by supplying an email address.

- **Class 2** – These certificates require additional personal information to be supplied.

- **Class 3** – These certificates can only be purchased after checks have been made about the requestor's identity.

- **Class 4** – They may be used by governments and financial organizations needing very high levels of trust.

Registration Authority (RA)

o CA may use a third-party Registration Authority (RA) to perform the necessary checks on the person or company requesting the certificate to confirm their identity. The RA may appear to the client as a

CA, but they do not actually sign the certificate that is issued.

Certificate Management System (CMS)

o It is the management system through which certificates are published, temporarily or permanently suspended, renewed, or revoked. Certificate management systems do not normally delete certificates because it may be necessary to prove their status at a point in time, perhaps for legal reasons. A CA along with associated RA runs certificate management systems to be able to track their responsibilities and liabilities.

Private Key Tokens

o While the public key of a client is stored on the certificate, the associated secret private key can be stored on the key owner's computer. This method is generally not adopted. If an attacker gains access to the computer, he can easily gain access to private key.

o For this reason, a private key is stored on secure removable storage token access to which is protected through a password.

o Different vendors often use different and sometimes proprietary storage formats for storing keys. For example, Entrust uses the proprietary .epf format, while Verisign, GlobalSign, and Baltimore use the standard .p12 format.

Hierarchy of CA

With vast networks and requirements of global communications, it is practically not feasible to have only one trusted CA from whom all users obtain their certificates. Secondly, availability of only one CA may lead to difficulties if CA is compromised.

In such case, the hierarchical certification model is of interest since it allows public key certificates to be used in environments where two communicating parties do not have trust relationships with the same CA.

- The root CA is at the top of the CA hierarchy and the root CA's certificate is a self-signed certificate.

- The CAs, which are directly subordinate to the root CA (For example, CA1 and CA2) have CA certificates that are signed by the root CA.

- The CAs under the subordinate CAs in the hierarchy (For example, CA5 and CA6) have their CA certificates signed by the higher-level subordinate CAs.

Certificate authority (CA) hierarchies are reflected in certificate chains. A certificate chain traces a path of certificates from a branch in the hierarchy to the root of the hierarchy.

The following illustration shows a CA hierarchy with a certificate chain leading from an entity certificate through two subordinate CA certificates (CA6 and CA3) to the CA certificate for the root CA.

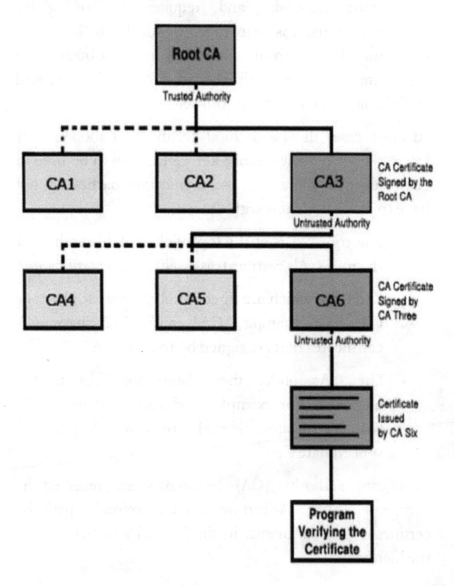

Verifying a certificate chain is the process of ensuring that a specific certificate chain is valid, correctly signed, and trustworthy. The following procedure verifies a certificate chain, beginning with the certificate that is presented for authentication –

- A client whose authenticity is being verified supplies his certificate, generally along with the chain of certificates up to Root CA.

- Verifier takes the certificate and validates by using public key of issuer. The issuer's public key is found in the issuer's certificate which is in the chain next to client's certificate.

- Now if the higher CA who has signed the issuer's certificate, is trusted by the verifier, verification is successful and stops here.

- Else, the issuer's certificate is verified in a similar manner as done for client in above steps. This process continues till either trusted CA is found in between or else it continues till Root CA.